I0484715

MARKETING
MANAGEMNENT

:: Author ::

ASHOKKUMAR D. PATEL

(M.COM., SLET)

PUBLISHED BY

Chakravarti Sidhdhharaj Jaysinh International
Publishing House
HQ. At & Po. Chaveli., Ta- Chansma,
Dist- Patan, North Gujarat, India, Asia.
www.iphouseindia.com

CORPORATE SOCIAL RESPONSIBILITY

First Publication: 18TH FEBRUARY, 2015

Copyright: Author
(c) ASHOKKUMAR D. PATEL

ISBN:- 978-15-08712-51-0

Price: Rs.750/- INDIA
       $ 15 OUTSIDE INDIA

PUBLISHED BY

Chakravarti Sidhdhharaj Jaysinh International
 Publishing House
HQ. At & Po. Chaveli., Ta- Chansma,
Dist- Patan, North Gujarat, India, Asia.
www.iphouseindia.com

Dedicated
to
my
Parents

Defining Marketing for the 21st Century

The 21st century has seen the advent of the new economy, thanks to the technology innovation and development. To understand the new economy, it is important to understand in brief characteristics and features of the old economy. Industrial revolution was the start point of the old economy with focus on producing massive quantities of standardized products. This mass product was important for cost reduction and satisfying large consumer base, as production increased companies expanded into new markets across geographical areas. The old economy had the organizational hierarchy where in top management gave out instructions which were executed by the middle manager over the workers.

In contrast, the new economy has seen the buying power at all time thanks to the digital revolution. Consumers have access to all types' information for product and services. Furthermore, standardization has been replaced by more customization with a dramatic increase in terms of product offering. Purchase experience has also changed as well with the introduction of online purchase, which can be done 24 × 7 with products getting delivered at office or home.

Companies have also taken advantage of information available and are designing more efficient marketing programs across consumers as well as the distribution channel. Digital revolution has increased speed of communication mobile, e-mail SMS, etc. This helps companies take faster decisions and implement strategies more swiftly.

Marketing is art of developing, advertising and distributing goods and services to consumer as well as business. However, marketing is not just limited to goods and services it is extended to everything from places to ideas and in between. This brings forth many challenges within which marketing people have to take strategy decisions. And answer to these challenges depends on the market the company is catering to, for consumer market decision are with respect to product, packaging and distribution channel. For business market, knowledge and awareness of product is very essential for marketing people as businesses are on the lookout to maintain or establish a credential in their respective market. For global market, marketing people have to consider not only culture diversity but also be careful with respect to international trade laws, trade agreement, and regulatory requirements of individual market. For non for profit organization with limited budgets, importance is related to pricing of products, so companies have to design and sell products accordingly.

Marketing philosophy employed by any given company has to be mix of organization interest, consumer interest and societal interest. In production philosophy, companies focus is on numbers, high production count, which reduces cost per unit and along with mass distribution. This kind of concept is usually making sense in a developing market where there is the need of product in large numbers. The product philosophy talks about consumers who are willing to pay an extra premium for high quality and reliable performance, so companies focus on producing well made products. The selling concept believes in pushing consumers into buying of products, which under normal circumstance, they would be resistant. The marketing concept believes consumer satisfaction, thereby developing and selling products keeping focus solely on customer needs and wants. The customer philosophy believes in the creation of customized products, where in products is design looking at historical transaction of consumers. The last philosophy is the societal concept which believes in developing products, which not only generate consumer satisfaction but also take into account well being of society or environment.

Digital revolution and 21st century have made companies fine tune the way they conduct their business. One major trend observed is the need of stream lining processes and systems with the focus on cost reduction through outsourcing. Another trend observed in companies is, encouragement to entrepreneur style of work environment with glocal (global-local) approach. At the same time, marketers of companies are looking forward to building long term relationship with consumers. This relationship establishes platform understanding consumer needs and preference. Marketers are looking at distribution channels as partners in business and not as the customer. Companies and marketers are making decisions using various computers simulated models.

To summarize 21st century marketing is challenge, which is to keep up pace with changing time.

Adapting Marketing to the New Economy

Companies in 21st century have to adapt to ever changing environment. At present, companies represent a curious mix of old as well as the new economy. A great deal of research has already been done with respect to the old economy, but for the new economy, companies are learning it rather hard way. Companies have to choose elements from old and new economy wisely as to build a business model which would bring value to the company.

Technology revolution, globalization and market deregulation factors are among many sculpting the new economy. These 3 factors interact with each other at different levels creating the driving force for the new economy. The old economy was full of analog devices, which were running on a continuous signal wave, for example, gramophone records. In today's world systems and devices are running on digital technology where information is carried in ones and zeroes. However, this digital information cannot be exchanged between devices without connectivity through wire or wireless networks. This connectivity is achieved through intranet, extranet and internet.

Internet allowed players like Yahoo, Amazon, ebay to offer products like music, books, apparel, etc. directly to customers. This move de-stabilized the traditional distributors and retailers causing some to shut down their business.

However, some of the players developed online portals to offer their products and services which in turn de-stabilized new online players. Some of the old players were successful with help of their brand strength and poor business models of pure online players.

In the old economy focus was only on standardization, mass production and singular marketing policy. However, with the amount of information available in the new economy, companies are best at understanding consumers. This better understanding has led to customized products, a shift from standardization. However, this customization has its drawbacks not only for companies but also for customer. Companies find it difficult to maintain the cost level for customized products to register profit. Customization is impossible for products, which require complex industrial engineering. Customer does not know real product appearance until it fully completed and also return policy is not there in customization.

The new functioning of economy has changed the way companies approach their business. Companies are looking forward to expanding across market segments to get maximum market share while keeping focus strictly on customer needs. For these companies are making organizational changes where departments are developed to manage a segment rather than a product. Companies are looking forward to developing consumer based brand equity to foster long term relation. Companies are coming up with products, which perform superior than consumer expectation there by creating a strong brand while the earlier branding task was accomplished through advertising. Companies are treating employees, distribution channel, and suppliers as their business partner and not customer.

Since companies have changed the way they function in the new economy, it is imperative that marketing practices also adapt. As consumers are looking forward going online for major of their purchase, businesses are looking towards electronic commerce (e-commerce) as a way forward. Research has shown online users usually buy music, software, books, apparel, etc. rather than goods like automobiles, house, etc. Business buyers are also coming online as well as suppliers, thereby substantially reducing the establishment cost. E-Commerce has also open doors for customer to customer relation through social networking and community forums, in which experience and discussion are done with respect to products. Through internet consumers are able to provide faster feedback to companies with respect to products and services.

As businesses are moving online, the focus shifts to developing of web sites to provide reliable and correct experience to consumers. Web site design, maintenance and security are of paramount importance for creating a favorable impression on consumer. Online marketing and advertisement have got prominence in this internet age.

The new economy had brought forward challenges and opportunities not only for companies but also for consumer.

Building Customer Satisfaction, Value and Retention

In this world of extreme competition, companies with a total focus on customer are going to be the winner. Companies must understand importance of customer satisfaction and then build process around it. A satisfied customer will be a loyal customer.

There are large offering of products and services available in the market then why the customer should choose a given company's product. According to various research and studies it has been confirmed that consumer will purchase products, which given them maximum perceived value. This value comes from calculating the cost associated with the emotional level decision like the brand image, corporate brand, sales personnel image and functional image. This value converts to total customer cost by including purchase cost, time-energy in evaluation of product and intuitive cost. Consumer will take decisions after considering the total cost associated with purchase, perceived and otherwise. If after the purchase product performs as expected than customer is considered satisfied. A completely satisfied customer is likely to repurchase the product and even promote the product through a word of mouth.

Companies are aiming for total customer satisfaction, which can be achieved after understanding customer expectation and then delivering as per the expectation. Companies are able to achieve this state of total customer satisfaction by incorporating good business practices. These practices are constructed around stakeholders, business process, resource and organization. Company's stakeholders consist of employees, suppliers, distributors and customers. Earlier focus has always solely been on shareholders, but now stakeholders need to be satisfied for shareholder's profit.

Companies need to define boundaries of relation with stakeholders as to get maximum value for every participant. To ensure maximum value, companies need to develop business processes, which understand and fulfill customer expectations. This can be achieved by aligning cross functional teams across critical processes, to create one smooth flow. Companies need to understand its core competencies and develop them, thereby successfully managing its resources. Organizational structure, design and policies have to be suitable to facilitate the introduction of total customer satisfaction culture.

Companies through creating and delivering value can develop total customer satisfaction. Company itself can be considered as a value chain consisting of primary and secondary activities. Primary activities consist of inbound materials, operation, delivering finished products, sales/marketing and servicing clients. Secondary activities consist of functional departments like technology department, procurement department, human resource and finance department. This value created is delivered to customer through the distribution channel under the principle of supply chain management.

Customers in the digital age are much more conscious and aware of their need and wants, making them a difficult lot to please. Companies run marketing campaign highlighting points of similarity and difference with competitor's products. The art is not at attracting the customer, but it is at retaining the customer and creating long term relation with them. Companies usually suffer from churning effect where customers do not make the repurchase. Companies need to work hard in identifying reasons behind this churning. Once reasons are identified separate them on the basis of manageable and non-manageable issues and then work hard at eliminating manageable issues.

Companies need to develop policies and measure at retaining customers along with attracting new customers. This art of retention can be achieved through customer relationship management (CRM). In CRM the task is to develop strong consumer based brand equity, which is done by converting first time buyer to repeat buyer to a client to a member to advocates and finally to partners. During these course companies can look forward to offering financial benefits in terms of discount for frequent buyers or also by association with a social cause.

Companies are in business to make the profit. Therefore, it has to identify profitable customers. Profitable customers provide a revenue stream more than the expense stream on retaining them. And this revenue stream should be higher for a company to have a competitive advantage. More and more companies are deploying total quality management approach across the organization to build and deliver customer satisfaction.

Gathering Information and Measuring Market Demand

In this dynamic market with the free flow of information and innovative marketing programs, needs and wants of consumers are always changing. As per capita income increases consumers are willing to explore more alternatives for purchase decision. Companies should be aware of changing situation all the time to take the right decision. This calls for development of sophisticated marketing information systems.

The information system consists of stakeholders, process and equipment to collect, analyze and proliferate information across relevant decision makers. The system is formulated using the internal company records, market research data and other intelligence gathering system. The internal system consists of analyzing information from product order to the delivery cycle and sales information systems. In product order to the delivery system, companies analyze consumption of various brands and make sure inventory of raw materials as well as finished products are maintained at sufficient levels. This is to make sure that whole cycle is completed in the shortest time possible. In the sales information systems, sales figure across different geographical centers are collected and analyzed to understand the consumption pattern. The data collected from the above process is analyzed to understand consumer behavior and develop products as well as programs to cater to consumer demand.

The marketing intelligence system requires a combination of people, system and procedure to gather market data. For the company, sales people are on the frontline to spot and report any trend prevailing in the market. The distribution channel also can provide companies with valuable information of the end user. However, sales people as well as distribution have to be train about spotting trends and then sending to the right people in the organization. Sometimes companies send a decoy into to the supermarket as a potential customer to check customer service, another way of gathering intelligence.

Companies also outsource intelligence gathering activities to agencies like A C Nielson.

If the marketing information system reports any issue or emerging trend then further analysis can be done through marketing research. The marketing research process consists of following; defining the problem, developing research plan, collecting data, analyzing data, presenting findings and implementing the decision. Each step has to be carefully planned and executed for market research to succeed. During problem defining process companies have to make sure that objective is not too vague, nor does it take researchers in the wrong direction. Developing research plan consist of creating a blue print as to how the information collection is going to occur. Here particular focus has to be maintained on cost for not over shoot the benefits. The step includes reaching out to the target audience and collecting information. Market researchers have various techniques and models at their disposal to analyze the collected data. Once market researchers are done with their analysis, findings have to be presented in a structure format as to answer the research objective questions. It is now for the top management to take the decision as the way forward from market research study.

In the world driven by technology, marketing managers are also making efforts to use the available resources. Marketing managers are routinely using the statistical tools like regression analysis, factor analysis, etc., models like markov process model, sales response models to support decision making process. Marketing managers are also using marketing and sales software, which helps in making day to day decision like pricing, budgeting, etc.

Once managers are able to finalize opportunities using marketing research and other technology backed models then next step forward is to calculate the market size, growth and other business model related attributes. Managers estimate market demand for a given product by calculating total product sell per market segment, per defined customer set, in a finite time and under specific marketing strategy. From these managers calculate company's market share vis-à-vis the competitor's business plan.

Marketing managers have to admit it is the consumer's market, which makes it important to gather information to understand their perception through available technology, market research and quantitative models. Understanding customers would help companies estimate total market demand for its products.

Scanning the Market Environment

under the influence of a number of factors to which company's stakeholders are participants. Some of the factors are as follows; globalization is affecting the way companies are conducting their business. Communication and connectivity are reaching at a new level every day. New economic powers like India, China, Brazil and Russia are exerting their influence. There are many other factors beyond the above mention which affect business working making it essential for companies to scan market condition.

Fad is short lived mushrooming of opportunity which is difficult to predict and forecast. Business profit from fad is pure matter of luck and chance. Trend is something which takes time to build up compared to fad and has a predictable future. Trend is sometimes co-related with changes in social culture and economical situation. Megatrend is much slower in development and is associated with political, socio-economical, technology and regulatory changes. Megatrends are estimated to last around half decade or more. For companies trend and megatrend are of great importance because they present business opportunities to them. Currently portable music player and hand held devices are real craze in the market with consumer willing to pay premium for them. However the direction in which market is going to develop is only possible by continuous following of market.

This trend-spotting activity can be undertaken by company itself or through market research. This activity can also be outsourced to companies, which specialize in analyzing current social and economical changes. Fitness and diet are another trend, which witness growth across the globe.

Factors influencing the market can be categorized under 6 different titles, demographic, economic, ecology, technology, regulatory-political and society-culture.

1. **Demographic factors:** are associated with changing nature and volume of population. It follows how people are conducting themselves in the new world, increasing per capita income, urban migration, ethnically diverse cities and mega cities. These are some demographic factors companies are monitoring. For example, a country like India and China are showing highest

concentration of youth population where as Japan is showing high number of retired workers. Therefore, demand and consumption of product will also be different.

2. **Economic factors:** deals with function like purchasing power parity, income level, savings level and interest rates among many other. For example, countries with a high income level are more likely to afford luxury items compare to a low income level country. Savings level and interest rate determine the borrowing power as well as spending power of consumer.

3. **Ecological factors:** consist of natural resource composition in a given county. For example, demand for fossil fuel has sky rocketed in recent years there by increasing general price level in the market. Companies, therefore, are looking forward to designing products which eco-friendly design that is they are less fuel dependent and give out less pollution.

4. **Technology factors:** like internet and connectivity are changing the face of business. More and more people are doing business online. Science and medicine are also part of technology factors. Challenge for the company is to

keep up with innovation and offer products, which are not obsolete.

5. **Political environment:** is also changing with more and more market based system rather than the socialist system. Furthermore, regulatory requirements like competition policy, investment policy, tax policy, etc. companies should investigate before taking their business to a particular country.

6. **Culture environment:** deals with factors like opinion people have towards themselves, others, organization and society in general. People have become more eco conscious, contributing one or many causes they can relate to, want organization to be responsible for their action and are looking to open society with meaningful co-existence.

All this 6 factors define any market environment and companies must understand them before developing their business plan.

Analyzing Consumer's Buying Behaviour

The core function of the marketing department is to understand and satisfy consumer need, wants and desire.

Consumer behaviour captures all the aspect of purchase, utility and disposal of products and services. In groups and organization are considered within the framework of consumer. Failing to understand consumer behaviour is the recipe for disaster as some companies have found it the hard way. For example, Wal-Mart launched operations in Latin-America with store design replicating that of US markets. However, Latin America consumer differs to US consumer in every aspect. Wal-Mart suffered consequences and failed to create impact.

Social, cultural, individual and emotional forces play a big part in defining consumer buying behaviour. Cultural, sub-culture and social class play an important is finalizing consumer behaviour. For example, consumer growing up in US is exposed to individualism, freedom, achievement, choice, etc. On sub-culture level influence of religion, race, geographic location and ethnicity define consumer behaviour. Social class consists of consumer with the same level of income, education, taste, feeling of superiority and inferiority. Over time consumer can move from one social level to another.

Culture alone cannot define consumer behaviour; social forces also play an important role. Social forces consist of family, friends, peer groups, status and role in society. Groups which have direct or indirect influence on consumer are referred to as reference groups. Primary groups consist of friends, family and peers with whom consumer has direct contact for considerable time. Secondary groups are association where interaction is at formal level and time devoted is less.

Consumer buying behaviour is influenced by individual's own personality traits. These personality traits do not remain the same but change with the life cycle. The choice of occupation and corresponding income level also play part in determining consumer behaviour. A doctor and software engineer both would have different buying pattern in apparel, food automobile etc. Consumers from similar background, occupation and income levels may show a different lifestyle pattern.

An individual buying behaviour is influenced by motivation, perception, learning, beliefs and attitude. These factors affect consumer at a psychological level and determine her overall buying behaviour. Maslow's hierarchy, Herzberg

Theory and Freud Theory try and explain people different motivational level in undertaking a buying decision. Perception is what consumer understands about a product through their senses. Marketers have to pay attention to consumer's perception about a brand rather than true offering of the product. Learning comes from experience; consumer may respond to stimuli and purchase a product. A favorable purchase will generate positive experience resulting in pleasant learning. Belief is the pre-conceived notion a consumer has towards a brand. It is kind of influence a brand exerts on consumer. For example, there is a strong belief product coming through German engineering are quality products. Companies may take advantage of this belief and route their production through Germany.

Companies need to think beyond buying behaviour and analyze the actual buying process. Complex buying behaviour requires high involvement of buyers, as it is infrequent in nature, expensive, and they are significant differences among the available choice e.g. automobile. Grocery buying is referred to as habitual buying, which requires less involvement as few differences among brands, frequent and inexpensive. Buying process involves purchase need, decision makers, information search, alternatives evaluation, purchase decision and post purchase behaviour. Companies try hard to understand consumer experience and expectation at every stage of buying process. Marketers need to figure the right combinations which will initiate purchase need e.g. marketing programs. Companies should ensure consumer have readily available information to take the decision e.g. internet, friends. Consumers evaluate alternatives based on their brand perception and belief. Companies need to work hard to develop products, which match this perception and belief every time. Final purchase decision is taken looking other's perception of the brand. Post purchase if expectations meet actual performance consumer is satisfied and more likely to repurchase or recommend the brand to others.

Consumer markets are defined by various geographical, social and cultural factors. Furthermore, consumer behaviour is influenced by psychological, personality, reference groups and demographic reasons. Finally actual buying process involves complex process and cycle. Companies have to keep a tab on all three factors in formulating strategy.

Analyzing Business Markets and Business Buying Behaviour

A market consists of two parts consumer market and business market. Companies manufacture products for consumer market but business market is equally large and strong. Typical business markets consist of manufacturing plants, machinery, industrial equipments, etc. Companies need to study and analyze factors affecting business markets and business buying behaviour.

In a business market, organizations buy goods and services for production of goods and services. In terms of overall value business market is bigger than the consumer market. There are many characteristic which set business market apart from consumer markets. Business buyer base is smaller in comparison to consumer market. Consumer-supplier relationship is much stronger in a business market owing to few players in the field. Customer and supplier are very dependent on each for survival. For example, if car companies falter then tyre companies will suffer. So companies not only have to monitor business market but also pay attention to end consumer market. Buying for the business is a responsibility of purchase department which adheres to company rules and regulations. The buying decision is influenced by many players ranging from technical experts to the finance department. This means that sales people have to do multiple visits and present information to different departments. In business market there is no distribution channel, thereby reducing overhead cost.

From the above discussion it is clear that the business market functions differently from consumer markets. Buying decision especially is more complex owing to many players. If buying decision is a re-purchase than purchasing department would place the order with an old supplier. Companies keep a list of approved vendors from which they choose as per purchase requirement. If buying decision is a modification from previous order in terms of specifications, amount, price, etc. than companies' looks to have a discussion with suppliers. Purchase department may look to other suppliers for a modification order. If the buying decision is a new product or service than a lengthy process is followed with discussion and meeting between representatives from various departments. Business buying behaviour is influenced by economical, company, individual and interpersonal factors. Economical factors like regulatory changes, technology changes, competition, fiscal policy and monetary policy influence buying behaviour. Business buyers are active in tracking and analyzing economical factors. Company level factors also play a major role is deciding buying behaviour. Sales people have to pay importance in understanding how purchase department is organized and players in the department. More professional are joining purchasing department making buying decision scientifically driven to align with larger organizational goals. As inventory management is crucial, companies' prefer long term relation with suppliers. Many individuals from different departments are part of buying decision and it is important for sales people to understand personality traits of as many participants as possible. Geographical factor also influences buying behaviour as culture varies from country to country. Sales people should be acquainted with different cultures.

Actual buying process can be understood from products' perspective. If the product has less perceived value and cost than business buyer ask for the lowest prices and offer high volume order. Suppliers in turn offer standardize products at low prices. If the product has a high value and low cost business buyer look for additional service or attributes with low price. If the product has high value and cost than the business buyer look for branded product with an established reputation. Price is not a constraint for high value products. To which suppliers put forward strategic long term alliance to accommodate technology changes.

Buying process consists of following steps - purchase needs, requirement description, product specification, floating intent of purchase, selecting a supplier; confirm delivery modules and timely review of purchase.

Government and institutional buying differ from industrial buying because here products and services providers are offered for free or fee to a large audience. Such a buying process requires a great deal of paperwork and transparent bidding system.

It is clear from observing the above points that in business buying and consumer buying. Business suppliers have to adapt to changes and employ a different marketing strategy.

Competition Strategy - Dealing with the Competition

Consumer and business markets have distinct characteristics by which they function. Earlier, importance was given mainly in understanding customer and their business. But in this age of technology and globalization companies cannot afford to ignore competition. Many companies are lowering their cost by outsourcing production to Asian countries. Companies must keep an eye on strategies and marketing program undertaken by competitors, to remain successful.

Michael Porter's five force model is appropriate in identifying competitive forces, which affect business in any given environment. These five forces are the threat of companies from same segment, threat of new entrants in the segment, threat from substitute products, threat from the increase in consumer's bargaining power and threat from supplier's bargaining power. If in the same segment there are too many players, if the segment is reaching saturation, if no further scope of expansion than to continue operation is difficult for the company. If the entry barrier are few and far than it makes easy for companies to enter, making segment un-attractive but if the entry barriers are tough than the company is better off in entering the segment. Substitute products are big threat and limit scope of a price increase. If

If consumers are better organized, have a choice in terms of product available and can create pressure on profits, making segment un-attractive. Similarly, if suppliers are better organized, less in number and supply is a key raw material for final output than also segment is unattractive.

Dealing with threats is one thing but if companies are not able to identify their competition than it can cause serious consequences. In recent years technology and internet have change the way business is conducted. Many companies were caught napping with respect to competition coming from the internet. Retailers like Wal-Mart and Target are facing competition from online retailer Amazon.com. Companies see competition in a direct format. This direct format consists of industry structure, number of players, entry-exit barriers, business model and ability to globalize. Market looks at competition in much more holistic manner where different products can satisfy a similar need. For example, for teens fashion can be explained by apparel to a music player, so with limited budget choice can only be one. Market approach increases the number of competitor in a real and abstract manner.

Companies after going through the process of identifying competition, also need to do in-depth analyze in terms of nature, strategy, strength, weakness and operation pattern. Companies following similar strategy need to group existing player in a matrix of product offering. For example, in the laptop market, apple is on the high end where as Dell offers low end models. Companies need to understand competitor's motive and goal to be in the market. US companies believe in shareholder value where as Japanese companies believe in market share. Next companies need to understand competitor's strength and weakness. For example, GM has good reach in USA but its weakness is quality where as Toyota does not have extensive dealer network but offers quality. Competitor's operating pattern also need careful study like competitor's action in the face of challenge to their position in the market.

To deal with competition companies need to design an intelligence system. Companies need to identify parameters which will help in analyzing the competition. It is then followed by gathering information for which source and methodology have to be finalized. Once the information is collected it has to be analyzed and sent to appropriate decision makers to act upon. As there are cost involved in design and maintaining such system, some companies give out contracts to companies which specialize in intelligence gathering activity.

The information from system is helpful in designing marketing strategies. Marketing strategy evolve depending on company position in the market. Market leaders, market challenger, market follower and niche players are four types of position strategy companies follow.

Dealing with competition is not an easy task and it requires dedicated resources of manpower, system and budget. Any lapse from company would result in decrease of market share and profit.

Positioning and Differentiating the Market Offering Through Product Life Cycle

Today's markets represent the surplus market, with a wide range of product available for sell. Consumer has huge product offering to choose from, for soap, there are more than dozen brands and each brand has at least 4 or 5 varieties. Companies have to work on strategies, which would differentiate their products from competitors. This differentiation strategy also cannot last for long as competition is likely to catch very soon. Companies are aware of the product life cycle; challenge is to work up strategies for positioning and differentiating as to extend product life and making it profitable.

A market place has many segments out of which companies have to make a choice in which to operate. And within the market segment companies need to decide its offering and image. This process of identifying and build the brand image within a segment as to occupy presence in consumer mind is called positioning. Positioning is all about consumers rather than the product, the challenge is to develop a positive perception in consumer mind. Positioning is done based on an idea the product promotes, too many ideas will confuse the customer. Companies need to decide which idea to promote to be ahead of completion. Positioning should offer clarity to customer about what product is all about. For example, a competitor has similar positioning ideas, than the company is better positioning product where it enjoys a competitive advantage. Now, it is up to the marketing plan to create programs which highlight this positioning idea.

Positioning related marketing programs are responsible to pass unique selling proposition on to the customer. However, this can be taken forward with differentiation.

Differentiation is process of adding more meaning to the product by highlighting attributes beyond the central theme. Task of differentiation is to highlight the relevant benefits in a distinctive manner which cannot be easily followed by competitors and provide profitable benefits to the company.

There are many differentiation tools available to the company to extract maximum benefits. The main variables which offer differentiation are product, service, personnel, channel and image. Product related attributes serve a good base of the differentiation. However, product differentiation varies depending on the nature of industry. For example, commodity products are difficult to differentiate on appearance where as automobiles present an opportunity with plenty of differentiations.

Service plays important differentiation tool where differentiation is difficult based on physical attributes of product. Differentiation in service can be achieved based on ordering ease, customer service during the sell, after sell customer service and consulting. One step forward in service is differentiation by personnel. By exhibiting a professional, reliable, quick and courteous response to customer can differentiate companies from competitors.

The distribution channel plays its part as differentiation tool and can prove to be competitive advantage. For example Dell computer through direct selling approach delivers computer system right at door step of home owners and offices.

Another important differentiation tool is image. There are various ways to achieve image differentiation depending on industry and market segment. Sponsoring of event and causes is one way building up image among consumers.

As pointed out earlier, company's strategy has to change according to the stage in the product life cycle. The product life has introduction stage, growth stage, maturity stage and saturation stage. In introduction stage focus is on establishing a foothold in the market space and consumer mind, through promotion, product trial and establishing distribution channel. In growth stage, sales are increasing and company is striving for the number one space. Strategies here consist of acquiring new customer, expansion brand line and fighting of competition. In maturation stage, growth is not explosive as before, there are no further distributors to add and sales start a decline. Here companies attempt to streamline product category, enter new markets and modify product feature as well as attributes. In saturation stage, it is time for companies to review sustainability of product by conducting the cost benefit analysis and remove products, which are dragging on company's profitability.

Markets in which companies are operating too have similar phases as products. Companies have to analyze positioning and differentiating strategies at various stages of the product and market life cycle.

Product Development Process - Developing New Market Offerings

Companies first find the target market than segment and then customers. After these companies go about developing products, which may be product modification or it may be a completely new product. Product offerings are increasing every year as consumers are looking for more and more variety of products. Companies which are unable to churn out new products fall back on competition and suffer the consequences. Companies face danger not just from competitors but consumer needs, technology, and product life cycle. New product development has its share of challenges. Research shows that 95 percent of new products fail in USA and in Europe failure rate is 90 percent.

Organizational set up has to be conducive to support new product development. Foremost companies must allocate funds for research and development, the conventional way is the percent of sales technique. Others chose to allow employees dedicate a certain amount of work time on new product development. Companies next have to organize the process of development. This can be done by product managers with new product development experience or by cross functional team with members chosen from various departments having the knack of developing new products. Nowadays, companies are following stage process for product development.

1. The 1st stage is idea generation that is the search for new products. Companies pay a particular focus on customer needs and demands to decide on the new product. Idea generation can also be done by studying competitor's product. Companies try to learn why competitor's product ticks with consumer or what more customers want from that product. Companies also look at top management for idea generation. For example, Steve Jobs of Apple is known to participate actively in an idea

generation. Research groups comprising of scientist, patent holders, colleges and universities also serve as the base for idea generation.

2. The 2nd stage is idea screening. Not all new ideas proposed can be converted into products. Companies list ideas into three categories promising ideas, marginal ideas and rejects. Promising ideas are further process by screening committee to be ready for the next stage. Screening should avoid the error where good ideas are dropped due to bias towards the idea generator. Another commonly occurring error is encouragement to a commercially unviable idea. Therefore, extra precautions are necessary during the screening process.

3. The 3rd stage begins when ideas move into the development process. Here a product idea is converted into several product concepts. Out of several product concepts, the one which looks fit is then placed against competitors to finalize marketing and positioning strategy. Product concept is introduced to a focus group of customer in a form of proto-type to understand their reaction.

4. The 4th stage involves developing of marketing strategy for new product. The marketing strategy involves evaluation of market size, product demand, growth potential, profit estimate in first few years. Further marketing strategy plan is developed with the launch of product, selection of distribution channel and budgetary requirements for the 1st year.

5. The 5th stage involves the development of the business model around the new product. Business models start with estimation of sales, frequency of purchase, and nature of business. Next estimation of cost and expense involve in production and distribution of new product. In that basis profit estimations are reached. Discounted cash flow and other methods are used to understand feasibility of new product.

6. The 6th stage involves the actual production of new product. Here more than one possible product are created, from proto-type to finalized products are produced. Decisions are taken from operation point of view whether is technically and commercially feasible to continue production. If analysis is showing cost not within the estimate then project is abandoned.

7. The 7th stage involves market testing of new product. The new product is ready with brand name, packaging, price to capture space in consumer's mind.

8. The 8th stage involves launching of product across target market backed by a proper marketing and strategy plan. This stage is called commercialization phase.

Introduction of new product is part of survival technique for any firm. And with very high failure rate companies have to follow a scientific process to create new market offerings. Setting the Product and Branding Strategy

Marketing strategy of a company revolves around 4Ps - Product, Price, Place and Promotion. Companies devise a strategy by mixing the four. The most important among is the product. All the marketing push and promotion will go waste if the product is not able to deliver. To come out with winner product, companies have to understand target customers needs and requirements.

Product Classifications and Strategy

Anything which companies produce to satisfy particular needs and demands is referred to as a product. Product is a broad category ranging from physical goods, tourism to managing a celebrity.

A product can be classified as to be made of five levels as shown in the figure below:-

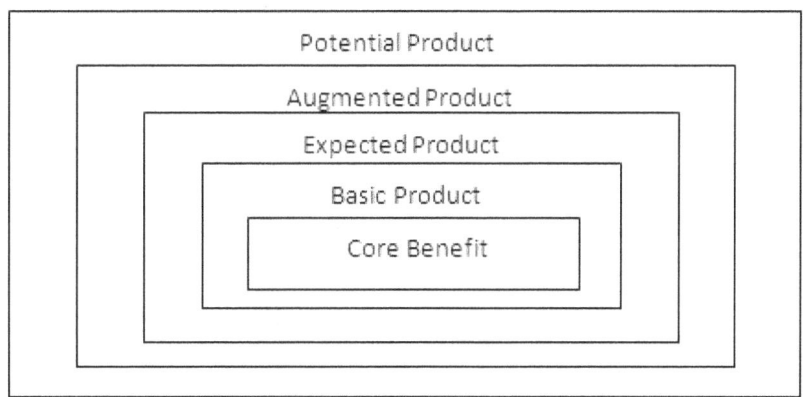

The core benefit is the underlying segment product is offering. For example, customer is buying commuting power when she purchases a car. Cars are fitted with comfortable seats, seat cover, and have desired color, converting a core product into the basic product. Companies are in business of providing value to products. At the expected level companies offer music system, child lock system and temperature control features. An augmented product provides more than customer expectation like a chrome wheels or sun/moon roof. However, augmentation increases the price of the product and customers have to pay extra. An augmented product gets converted into an expected. At potential level companies provides products considering all the possible augmentation.

The product itself is arranged in a hierarchy like need family, product family, product class, product line, product type and item based on needs it satisfies. Further product can be classified on durability, tangibility and usage. Durability comprises of durable and non-durable goods. Non-durable goods comprises of product like soap and beer, which are of frequent purchase and usually consumed quickly. These goods are available at many locations and require more allocation for advertising. Durable goods include TV, washing machines and music system. These goods require more personal touch for selling as the customer would like to understand all features and functions. Intangible products are in the form of services, like haircutting and car repair.

Product usage divides the product into industrial goods and consumer goods. Convenience goods are consumer goods, which can be bought by the customer without much fuss, for example, soaps, beer and newspaper. Shopping goods are type of consumer goods where in customer compare characteristics with other products in same category bases on price, quality and appearance, for example, clothing, furniture and used car. Specialty goods are type of consumer goods where consumers need to make extra efforts in purchasing them, for example, yacht or luxury car. Unsought goods are consumer goods, which are not part of daily life and routine, for example, smoke detectors and cemetery plots.

Industrial goods can be further classified into capital goods and regular business supply. Capital goods are type of industrial goods, which are required for production of final products, for example, plant and machinery. Business goods are type of industrial goods, which are required for day to day functioning as well as on special occasion, for example, office supplies, lubricants and spare parts.

Branding Strategy

Another important aspect of product strategy is branding. Branding is process of giving identity and image to the product as to create an impression in the mind of consumer. Branding is a long process involves lots of investments in terms of money and time from the company. Building brand identity involves designing name, symbol and logo for the product. Branding involves developing strategy to create a point of differentiation from competitors as well point of similarity with product class. Brand which reaches a high level of awareness and enjoys the loyalty from customer develops brand equity. Packaging of the products also forms part of branding strategy.

Creating a unique product identity and branding strategy is important in formulating success of the company. Customer's purchase decision will be based on attractive product and branding strategy.

Tools of Promotion - Advertising, Sales Promotion, Public Relation & Direct Marketing

The 4 Ps of marketing are product, price, place and promotion. All four of these elements combine to make a successful marketing strategy. Promotion looks to communicate the company's message across to the consumer. The four main tools of promotion are advertising, sales promotion, public relation and direct marketing.

Advertising

Advertising is defined as any form of paid communication or promotion for product, service and idea. Advertisement is not only used by companies but in many cases by museum, government and charitable organizations. However, the treatment meted out to advertisement defers from an organization to an organization.

Advertising development involves a decision across five Ms Mission, Money, Message, Media and Measurement.

Mission looks at setting objectives for advertising. The objectives could be to inform, persuade, remind or reinforce. Objective has to follow the marketing strategy set by the company.

Money or budget decision for advertising should look at stage of product life cycle, market share and consumer base, competition, advertising frequency and product substitutability.

Message's development further is divided into four steps, message generation, message evaluation and selection, message execution, and social responsibility review.

Once the message is decided the next step is finalizing the media for delivering the message. The choice of depends on reach of media, frequency of transmission and potential impact on customer. Based on this choice of media types are made from newspaper, television, direct mail, radio, magazine and the internet. After which timing of broadcast of the message is essential as to grab attention of the target audience. Checking on the effectiveness of communication is essential to company's strategy. There are two types of research communication effect research and sales effect research.

Sales Promotion

Promotion is an incentive tool used to drive up short term sales. Promotion can be launched directed at consumer or trade. The focus of advertising to create reason for purchase the focus of promotion is to create an incentive to buy. Consumer incentives could be samples, coupons, free trial and demonstration. Trade incentive could be price off, free goods and allowances. Sales force incentive could be convention, trade shows, competition among sales people.

Sales promotion activity can have many objectives, for example, to grab attention of new customer, reward the existing customer, increase consumption of occasional users. Sales promotion is usually targeted at the fence sitters and brand switchers.

Sales promotional activity for the product is selected looking at the overall marketing objective of the company. The final selection of the consumer promotional tools needs to consider target audience, budget, competitive response and each tool's purpose. Sales promotion activity should under-go pretest before implementation. Once the activity is launched it should be controlled as to remain within the budget. Evaluation program is a must after implementation of the promotional scheme.

Public Relations

Companies cannot survive in isolation they need to have a constant interaction with customers, employees and different stakeholders. This servicing of relation is done by the public relation office. The major function of the public relation office is to handle press releases, support product publicity, create and maintain the corporate image, handle matters with lawmakers, guide management with respect to public issues.

Companies are looking at ways to converge with functions of marketing and public relation in marketing public relation. The direct responsibility of marketing public relation (MPR) is to support corporate and product branding activities.

MPR is an efficient tool in building awareness by generating stories in media. Once the story is in circulation MPR can establish credibility and create a sense of enigma among sales people as well as dealers to boost enthusiasm. MPR is much more cost effective tool than other promotional activities.

Direct Marketing

The communication establishes through a direct channel without using any intermediaries is referred to as direct marketing. Direct marketing can be used to deliver message or service. Direct marketing has shown tremendous growth in recent years. The internet has played major part in this growth story. Direct marketing saves time, makes an experience personal and pleasant. Direct marketing reduces cost for companies. Face to face selling, direct mail, catalog marketing, telemarketing, TV and kiosks are media for direct marketing.

Advertisement, Promotional activity, Public relation and direct marketing play an essential role in helping companies reaches their marketing goals.

Managing the Sales Force

The face of any organization is the sales force. Companies spend a considerable amount of time and money on sales force rather than on any other promotional activity. However, sales force is expensive and companies are looking forward to managing them in an efficient and effective manner.

Designing of the Sales Force

Sales force is linking between companies and customer. Therefore, companies have to be careful in designing and structuring sales force.

1. The first step is setting out an objective for sales force. Earlier companies had a single objective increasing sale making it objective also for sales people. Sales people are asked to perform a search for prospective clients or lead. Sales people are asked to balance time between a prospective customer and current customer. Effective communication of product and services is essential to close the deal. Sales people also play an important role in after sales service and can make a difference for the company. Sales people are eyes and ears of the company in the market gathering information about competition and customer changing demands.

2. The second step is use sales people strategically. Sales people have to combine efforts with other team members to achieve the objective. Sales people should be aware how to analyze market data been provided and convert them into marketing strategies.

3. The third step is deciding the structure of the sales force. The structure of the sales is dependent on the strategy followed by the company. Common sales force structures are as follows:-

- Territorial structure is used where every sales representative is assigned specific geographical area. This structure is preferred for building relationships with locals.

- Product structure is used for complex and un-related product portfolio. Here the sales people are directly associated with research and development of the products.

- Market structure is used if the companies are operating different industry or market segments. Every sales force specializes in a definite market and helps push a product efficiently across the given market. However, the disadvantage would arise if customers are located over a wide geographical area.

- Complex structure is used when companies are in business of selling complex product to different customer across a large geographical area. Here sales force structure is a combination of other structures discussed.

Once the structure is designed companies need to make a decision with respect to the size of the sales force. The size of the sales force is dependent on the market size and number of customers.

4. The next step is to design compensation for the sales force. Compensation plays a big motivational factor for sales people. Companies follow a structure of a fixed amount plus a variable amount depending of success achieved in the market. Allowances play an important factor in the salary owing to continuous travel and market visits.

Managing Sales Force

Integral part for success of marketing strategy is management of the sales force. The management of sales consists of following:-

Recruitment is at the centre of an effective sales force. One approach in the selection is asking a customer what characteristics they look for in a sales representative. Companies develop selection procedure where behavioral and management skills are tested.

Training is essential to remain ahead of the competition. Sales force needs training before entering the market as well as training at different stage of the product life cycle. Supervision on sales force is decided on the profile of product portfolio. A general supervision is maintained with respect to sales people dealing with potential clients. Another supervision is related to efficient time management from preparation of client call to closing of the deal.

Motivation is a key aspect for management of the sales force. Here compensation plays an important in driving up the motivational level. Compensation can be assigned based on sales quota. Other motivational tools are social gathering and family outing.

Evaluation is essential to management of a sales force. Sales reports sent by the sales force serve a good starting point of evaluation. Art of negotiation and relationship marketing these two are the important aspects of successful sales representative and long term benefit for the company.

Facebook as a Digital Marketing Tool

Introduction

Digital Marketing entails marketing of goods and services using digital technologies and digital mediums. In this context it would be pertinent to note that with the advent of Web 2.0 or social media, marketers now have the chance to utilize the opportunities offered by digital marketing using social media like Facebook. This article explores the advantages and disadvantages of using Facebook for digital marketing and discusses the various issues surrounding this concept. Before launching into the discussion, it would be worthwhile to note that the unparalleled access to a large consumer base afforded by Facebook makes it the ideal medium of choice for marketers especially those in the business of consumer goods and FMCG or Fast Moving Consumer Goods. This is because Facebook has a combined user base of more than a billion people and reaches nearly one in four adults in the United States alone. Apart from this, the use of Facebook in the emerging markets is even more pervasive with estimates suggesting that out of the 80 percent of the total Facebook users who are from outside of the United States, nearly half of them are active users making the medium a platform for brands to be noticed in the "noisy social media world".

Advantages of Using Facebook

Continuing the points made above, it is indeed the case that Facebook offers penetration and reach to marketers especially those operating on shoestring budgets, as they do not have to spend large amounts of money on expensive marketing campaigns. Moreover, unlike traditional media where the effectiveness and efficacy of a marketing campaign cannot be measured directly and instead, readership or viewership metrics are used, Facebook marketing can be measured for its efficacy as click through and conversion of eyeballs into purchases is readily available. Further, Facebook offers the unprecedented chance for marketers to target a global audience and at the same time, consider local factors. In other words, what this means is that marketers can create campaigns, which have a global theme and at the same time can reach out to their local audience as well. the conflation of reaching out to a wider audience without compromising on the local customers means that Facebook becomes the social networking site of choice when compared to Twitter and Instagram that are more focused in their reach. Further, the "death of distance" and the removal of the geographical constraints mean that spatial and locational barriers are nonexistent with Facebook Digital Marketing. Already companies like Coca Cola and Starbucks have used the power of Facebook to integrate it with their marketing strategies for effective customer outreach.

Downsides of Using Facebook

Of course, there are downsides to using Facebook as a marketing tool and these include the rapidity with which negative publicity can travel around the world in a jiffy. For instance, a jealous competitor or a disgruntled employee might post negative comments or information about the brand or the product and considering the ways in which such comments can go "viral" in a matter of hours and even minutes, it is the case that marketers and companies have to be always on the lookout for what is being said and commented upon on their products. The point to be noted here is that by the time, the marketer, the company representative comes up with a rebuttal, or the disproving of the negative comment or publicity, the damage would have been done. Apart from this, using Facebook as the digital marketing medium means that instant gratification is the norm rather than any sustained engagement with the brand. This results in users (who are mostly of the Generation Y) forming opinions of the brand in a shallow and superficial manner which means that little attention is paid to deeper thought and nuanced marketing as is the case with traditional media.

Other issues to be considered

We have considered the advantages and disadvantages of using Facebook for Digital Marketing. Apart from these, other issues count in favor of Facebook. For instance, marketing on Facebook is easy and inexpensive when compared to traditional media as all one needs to do is to integrate Facebook into the company's online marketing strategy and create a fan page or a dedicated page in addition to providing for targeted messages aimed the focused consumer segment. Further, marketing on Facebook can bring additional benefits as can be seen in the company's recent moves to be more aggressive as far as e-Commerce and m-Commerce are concerned. This has long been a sticking point between Facebook and its corporate clients, as the latter wanted the former to integrate these aspects more into the overall strategy.

Conclusion

Before concluding this article, one must consider the fact that news travels fast in the online world and travels instantaneously in the social media world. Therefore, this can be a force for good and at the same time, can yield unpredictable results. Moreover, integrating Facebook into a company's overall marketing strategy must be done only after due diligence is done as the cost benefit analysis works differently for different companies in the different sectors. In conclusion, Facebook is a game changer for marketers and the emerging trends indicate that it would be used more by the marketers as they seek more bang for the buck in terms of the returns per dollar spent on marketing and advertising.

The Art of Strategic Marketing: Market Learning, Sensing, and Intuiting

Market Learning

The first step in strategic marketing is to learn from the market about the changing consumer preferences and attitudes. Firms typically employ market research agencies to conduct surveys and research reports about how consumers

and their preferences goods and services over others are changing with the times. In other words, firms attempt to understand the market by direct observation by surveying the consumers and finding out what they would buy. Apart from this, market learning also involves direct interaction with the consumers to try and understand why they prefer a certain brand to others. The strategies that the firm adopts after the market learning process are based on the feedback that they have received from the ground. This kind of strategizing is quite popular with marketers and practitioners of strategic marketing as it helps them fine tune their strategies based on market preferences.

Market Sensing

This approach deals with going a step ahead of market learning and combining data and experience to understand how the market moves. In other words, after the data collection is done, marketers who are experienced or talented put the data and the strategic models of marketing together and try and sense how the market moves. For those who follow the stock markets, the term "mood of the market" and "market sentiment" is terms that can be known as sensing how the market moves based on both data and the wisdom of accumulated experience.

Market Intuiting

We have discussed how firms try and understand consumer preferences by direct observation and by an indirect analytical method of "sensing" how the market would move.

The third aspect in this sub-topic of strategic marketing takes the whole concept ever further by adopting what can be called as "Market Intuiting". In other words, this approach involves to know the "mind and soul of the market" and to predict the future based on both data and an intuitive understanding of how the market would move. Lest one thinks that this approach is like Astrology or other such forms of prediction, there have been the cases of marketers like the late legendary Steve Jobs who could "feel it in his gut" about how consumers would either flock to the brands or abandon it altogether. The idea in this approach is to "preempt" the future by preparing for it and as the saying goes, chance favors the prepared mind. Hence, after studying the market through direct observation, sensing the mood of the market, this third approach is to get into the very essence of the consumer, which is to do with how he or she would behave in the future.

Closing Thoughts

The key aspect here is that in the fast changing business landscape of the 21st century, it is not merely enough to measure data and proceed accordingly. On the other hand, the consumer behavior, which is in a flux, cannot be sensed by experience alone. Hence, the combination of the strategies outlined here can be followed to beat the expectations of the consumers and by gaining insights into the mind of the consumer and getting inside their heads, marketers can hope to outclass the competition.

Advertising Management

Advertising simply put is telling and selling the product. Advertising Management though is a complex process of employing various media to sell a product or service. This process begins quite early from the marketing research and encompasses the media campaigns that help sell the product. Without an effective advertising management process in place, the media campaigns are not that fruitful and the whole marketing process goes for a toss. Hence, companies that believe in an effective advertising management process are always a step ahead in terms of selling their goods and services.

As mentioned above, advertising management begins from the market research phase. At this point, the data produced by marketing research is used to identify what types of advertising would be adequate for the specific product. Gone are the days when there was only print and television advertising was available to the manufacturers. These days apart from print and television, radio, mobile, and Internet are also available as advertising media. Advertising management process in fact helps in defining the outline of the media campaign and in deciding which type of advertising would be used before the launch of the product.

If you wish to make the advertising effective, always remember to include it from the market research time. Market research will help to identify the niche segment of the population to which the product or service has to be targeted from a large population. It will also identify why the niche segment would opt for the product or service. This information will serve as a guideline for the preparation of advertising campaigns.

Once the niche segments are identified and the determination of what types of advertising will be used is done, then the advertising management focuses on creating the specifics for the overall advertising campaign. If it is a radio campaign, which type of ads would be used, if it is a print campaign, what write ups and ads will be used, and if it is a television campaign, what type of commercials will be used. There might also be a mix and match advertising in which radio might supplement television advertising and so on. It is important that through advertising management the image is conveyed that all the strategies complement each other. It should not look to public that the radio advertising is focusing on something else while television on something else. The whole process in the end should benefit the product or service.

The role of people designing the advertising campaign is crucial to its success. They have been trained by seasoned professionals who provide the training in the specific field. Designing an advertising campaign is no small a task and to understand the consumer behavior from the data collected from market research is a very important aspect of the campaign. A whole lot of creativity and inspiration is required to launch an adequate advertising campaign. In addition, the management skills come into play when the work has to be done keeping the big picture in mind. It would be fruitful for the company if the advertising campaign lasts well over the lifetime of a product or service, reach the right customers, and generate the desired revenue.

Steps in Advertising Process

"Mass demand has been created almost entirely through the development of Advertising"

Calvin Coolidge in the New York Public Library.

For the development of advertising and to get best results one need to follow the advertising process step by step.

The following are the steps involved in the process of advertising:

1. Step 1 - Briefing: the advertiser needs to brief about the product or the service which has to be advertised and doing the SWOT analysis of the company and the product.

2. Step 2 - Knowing the Objective: one should first know the objective or the purpose of advertising. i.e. what message is to be delivered to the audience?

3. Step 3 - Research: this step involves finding out the market behavior, knowing the competitors, what type of advertising they are using, what is the response of the consumers, availability of the resources needed in the process, etc.

4. Step 4 - Target Audience: the next step is to identify the target consumers most likely to buy the product. The target should be appropriately identified without any confusion.

For e.g. if the product is a health drink for growing kids, then the target customers will be the parents who are going to buy it and not the kids who are going to drink it.

5. Step 5 - Media Selection: now that the target audience is identified, one should select an appropriate media for advertising so that the customers who are to be informed about the product and are willing to buy are successfully reached.

6. Step 6 - Setting the Budget: then the advertising budget has to be planned so that there is no short of funds or excess of funds during the process of advertising and also there are no losses to the company.

7. Step 7 - Designing and Creating the Ad: first the design that is the outline of ad on papers is made by the copywriters of the agency, then the actual creation of ad is done with help of the art directors and the creative personnel of the agency.

8. Step 8 - Perfection: then the created ad is re-examined and the ad is redefined to make it perfect to enter the market.

9. Step 9 - Place and Time of Ad: the next step is to decide where and when the ad will be shown.

The place will be decided according to the target customers where the ad is most visible clearly to them. The finalization of time on which the ad will be telecasted or shown on the selected media will be done by the traffic department of the agency.

10.   Step 10 - Execution: finally the advertise is released with perfect creation, perfect placement and perfect timing in the market.

11.   Step 11 - Performance: the last step is to judge the performance of the ad in terms of the response from the customers, whether they are satisfied with the ad and the product, did the ad reached all the targeted people, was the advertise capable enough to compete with the other players, etc. Every point is studied properly and changes are made, if any. If these steps are followed properly then there has to be a successful beginning for the product in the market.

Advertising Techniques - 13 Most Common Techniques Used by the Advertisers

Today every company needs to advertise its product to inform the customers about the product, increase the sales, acquire market value, and gain reputation and name in the industry. Every business spends lot of money for advertising their products but the money spent will lead to success only when the best techniques of advertising are used for the product. So here are some very common and most used techniques used by the advertisers to get desired results.

1. Emotional Appeal

This technique of advertising is done with help of two factors - needs of consumers and fear factor. Most common appeals under need are:

- need for something new
- need for getting acceptance
- need for not being ignored
- need for change of old things
- need for security
- need to become attractive, etc.

Most common appeals under fear are:

- fear of accident
- fear of death
- fear of being avoided
- fear of getting sick
- fear of getting old, etc.

2. Promotional Advertising

This technique involves giving away samples of the product for free to the consumers. The items are offered in the trade fairs, promotional events, and ad campaigns in order to gain the attention of the customers.

3. Bandwagon Advertising

This type of technique involves convincing the customers to join the group of people who have bought this product and be on the winning side. For e.g. recent Pantene shampoo ad which says "15crores women trusted Pantene, and you?"

4. Facts and Statistics

Here, advertisers use numbers, proofs, and real examples to show how good their product works. For e.g. "Lizol floor cleaner cleans 99.99% germs" or "Colgate is recommended by 70% of the dentists of the world" or Eno - just 6 seconds.

5. Unfinished Ads

The advertisers here just play with words by saying that their product works better but don't answer how much more than the competitor. For e.g. Lays - no one can eat just one or Horlicks - more nutrition daily. The ads don't say who can eat more or how much more nutrition.

6. Weasel Words

In this technique, the advertisers don't say that they are the best from the rest, but don't also deny. E.g. Sunsilk Hairfall Solution - reduces hairfall. The ad doesn't say stops hairfall.

7. Endorsements

The advertisers use celebrities to advertise their products. The celebrities or star endorse the product by telling their own experiences with the product. Recently a diamond jewellery ad had superstar Amitabh Bacchan and his wife Jaya advertising the product. The ad showed how he impressed his wife by making a smart choice of buying this brand. Again, Sachin tendulkar, a cricket star, endorsed for a shoe brand.

8. Complementing the Customers

Here, the advertisers used punch lines which complement the consumers who buy their products. E.g. Revlon says "Because you are worth it."

9. Ideal Family and Ideal Kids

The advertisers using this technique show that the families or kids using their product are a happy go lucky family. The ad always has a neat and well furnished home, well mannered kids and the family is a simple and sweet kind of family. E.g. a dettol soap ad shows everyone in the family using that soap and so is always protected from germs. They show a florescent color line covering whole body of each family member when compared to other people who don't use this soap.

10.   Patriotic Advertisements

These ads show how one can support their country while he uses their product or service. For e. g some products together formed a union and claimed in their ad that if you buy any one of these products, you are going to help a child to go to school. One more cellular company ad had a celebrity showing that if the customers use this company's sim card, then they can help control population of the country.

11.   Questioning the Customers

The advertisers using this technique ask questions to the consumers to get response for their products. E.g.

Amway advertisement keeps on asking questions like who has so many farms completely organic in nature, who gives the strength to climb up the stairs at the age of 70, who makes the kids grow in a proper and nutritious ways, is there anyone who is listening to these entire questions. And then at last the answer comes - "Amway : We are Listening."

12.   Bribe

This technique is used to bribe the customers with some thing extra if they buy the product using lines like "buy one shirt and get one free", or "be the member for the club for two years and get 20% off on all services."

13.   Surrogate Advertising

This technique is generally used by the companies which cannot advertise their products directly. The advertisers use indirect advertisements to advertise their product so that the customers know about the actual product. The biggest example of this technique is liquor ads. These ads never show anyone drinking actual liquor and in place of that they are shown drinking some mineral water, soft drink or soda.

These are the major techniques used by the advertisers to advertise their product. There are some different techniques used for online advertising such as web banner advertising in which a banner is placed on web pages, content advertising using content to advertise the product online, link advertising giving links on different sites to directly visit the product website, etc.

Classification of Advertising

Advertising is the promotion of a company's products and services though different mediums to increase the sales of the product and services. It works by making the customer aware of the product and by focusing on customer's need to buy the product. Globally, advertising has become an essential part of the corporate world. Therefore, companies allot a huge part of their revenues to the advertising budget. Advertising also serves to build a brand of the product which goes a long way to make effective sales.

There are several branches or types of advertising which can be used by the companies. Let us discuss them in detail.

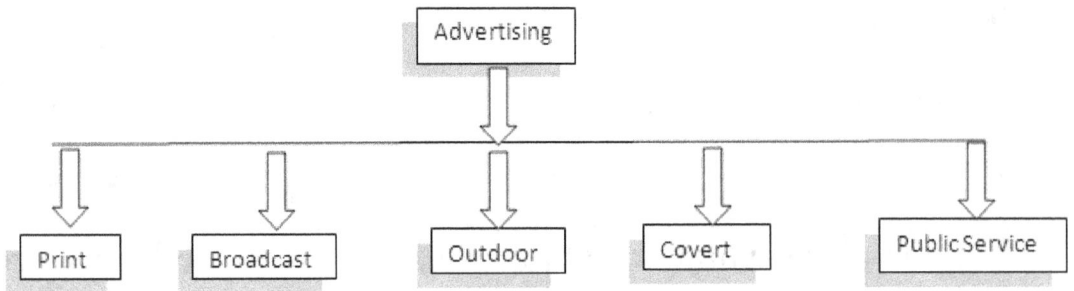

Classification of Advertising

1. **Print Advertising** - The print media has been used for advertising since long. The newspapers and magazines are quite popular modes of advertising for different companies all over the world. Using the print media, the companies can also promote their products through brochures and fliers. The newspaper and magazines sell the advertising space and the cost depends on several factors. The quantity of space, the page of the publication, and the type of paper decide the cost of the advertisement. So an ad on the front page would be costlier than on inside pages. Similarly an ad in the glossy supplement of the paper would be more expensive than in a mediocre quality paper.

2. **Broadcast Advertising** - This type of advertising is very popular all around the world. It consists of television, radio, or Internet advertising. The ads on the television

have a large audience and are very popular. The cost of the advertisement depends on the length of the ad and the time at which the ad would be appearing. For example, the prime time ads would be more costly than the regular ones. Radio advertising is not what it used to be after the advent of television and Internet, but still there is specific audience for the radio ads too. The radio jingles are quite popular in sections of society and help to sell the products.

3. **Outdoor Advertising -** Outdoor advertising makes use of different tools to gain customer's attention. The billboards, kiosks, and events and tradeshows are an effective way to convey the message of the company. The billboards are present all around the city but the content should be such that it attracts the attention of the customer. The kiosks are an easy outlet of the products and serve as information outlets for the people too. Organizing events such as trade fairs and exhibitions for promotion of the product or service also in a way advertises the product. Therefore, outdoor advertising is an effective advertising tool.

4. **Covert Advertising -** This is a unique way of advertising in which the product or the message is subtly included in a movie or TV serial. There is no actual ad, just the mention of the product in the movie. For example, Tom Cruise used the Nokia phone in the movie Minority Report.

5. **Public Service Advertising -** As evident from the title itself, such advertising is for the public causes. There are a host of important matters such as AIDS, political integrity, energy conservation, illiteracy, poverty and so on all of which need more awareness as far as general public is concerned. This type of advertising has gained much importance in recent times and is an effective tool to convey the message.

Print Advertising

Print advertising is a widely used form of advertising. These advertisements appear in newspapers or magazines and are sometimes included as brochures or fliers. Anything written in the print media to grab the attention of the specific target audience comes under the purview of print advertising. People who read newspapers or other publications have a tendency to browse the print ads that they come across. The decision to buy the product might not be instantaneous, but it does settle down in their subconscious mind. Next time they see the product in the market, they are tempted to buy it.

Print advertisements are only effective when people see them. When people browse through newspapers and publications, these advertisements should grab the attention of the potential customer. Therefore, these advertisements should be created in such a manner that they can hold the attention of the customer to some extent. Usually a team of individuals is required in order to design the advertisements.

The newspaper or magazine ad should be such that it should compel people to spend money on the products. This is just what the advertising team does. To create such an ad, the team members work on a concept and develop the wordings and images of the ad. These wordings and images are then brought together to form the final ad. Then there are people who deal with the placement of the ad. They have to make sure that if the client has paid for premium place, they get the desired exposure. For example, an ad on the first page will get instant attention of the reader than the ad on the subsequent pages. Likewise, an ad which occupies greater space is likely to get more attention. All these factors have to be looked into while designing the ad.

The sales team of the publication makes sure that it gets ads regularly. In fact, these ads are a major source of income for the publication and hence it is expected that there should be a constant flow of the ads. The sales team does just that. Mailers are another type of print ads. These can range from well-designed postcards to simple paper leaflets. These are usually delivered by the postal workers in people's mailboxes. The problem with these mailers is that they get least attention and are usually considered as junk and thrown away even without reading. To reduce this occurrence, companies sometimes make use of fliers. These are paper ads which are handed over to individuals in person. The logic is that if the ad is given to people personally, they will pay more attention to it, which is actually true to some extent.

Though print advertising is still very popular, it does take a hit from time to time. For example, during the recession phase, when people's budgets were tight, they did not resort to print ads. In addition, with the advent of Internet, the print ads in the publications have gone down because Internet has a wider reach online. To overcome this scenario, new strategies have to be developed by advertisers and the print media. Globally, advertisers keep on developing strategies which benefit the business of print publications. Therefore, it can be said that print advertising is here to stay.

Broadcast Advertising

Generally speaking, broadcast advertising is radio, television, and Internet advertising. The commercials aired on radio and televisions are an essential part of broadcast advertising.

The broadcast media like radio and television reaches a wider audience as opposed to the print media. The radio and television commercials fall under the category of mass marketing as the national as well as global audience can be reached through it.

The role of broadcast advertising is to persuade consumers about the benefits of the product. It is considered as a very effective medium of advertising. The cost of advertising on this channel depends on the time of the commercial and the specific time at which it is aired. For example, the cost of an ad in the premium slot will be greater than in any other slot.

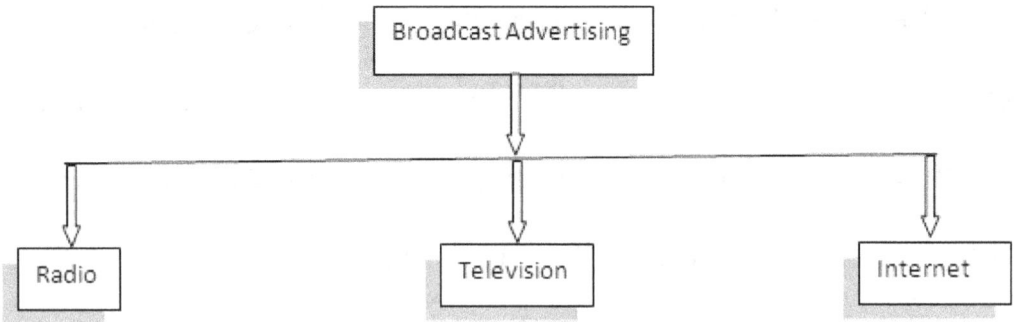

A radio ad must be aired several times before it actually sinks in the minds of the consumers. Thus the frequency of the ad is important. The type of your target audience is also important. Therefore, one must do a research on which type of audience listens to which channels if they want the ads to be successful. The voice talent in the commercial should be taken keeping in mind the type of audience and the type of commercial.

The television advertising is usually considered the advertising for the corporate giant, though even the small businesses can benefit from it. A strong audio and video combination is a must for the success of the commercial. But it is also important that the audio and video should function well without each other. For example, if a person is not viewing the TV but just listening to it, s/he should get the idea and vice versa.

It is extremely important that whatever has been advertised in the commercial is true. For this reason, organizations such as Federal Trade Commission (FTC) are there to monitor the commercials on television and radio. This ensures that the advertisers are not making any false claims to lure consumers to buy their products.

Most of the radio and television advertisements are paid though there are some public service ads which can be aired for free. The advertisers usually have to pay for the spot which lasts for 30 seconds. In rare cases, this spot can increase to 60 seconds too.

These days radio and television ads are prepared by advertising agencies for their clients. They understand the need of the client and make the commercial keeping in mind the current state of affairs. Broadcast advertising has become a very essential part of marketing in recent times. Companies allocate specific budget for radio and television ads and make an estimate of how much revenue they can earn through broadcast advertising. For example, marketing consultants are hired to determine the return on investment (ROI) for spending on radio and television ads. Sometimes the marketing consultants of these businesses run sample ads to judge its popularity among the viewers.

Internet or online advertising uses the Internet or the World Wide Web for the purpose of attracting consumers to buy their product and services. Examples of such advertising include ads on search engine result pages, rich media ads, banner ads, social network advertising, and email marketing and so on. Online advertising has its benefits, one of them being immediate publishing of the commercial and the availability of the commercial to a global audience. But along with the benefits come the disadvantages too. These days, advertisers put distracting flashing banners or send across email spam messages to the people on a mass scale. This can annoy the consumers and even the real ads might get ignored in the process. Therefore, ethics in advertising is very important for it to be successful.

Whatever the mode of advertising, broadcast advertising is an inherent part of any advertising campaign these days.

Outdoor Advertising

Outdoor advertising communicates the message to the general public through highway billboards, transit posters and so on. Outdoor advertising is a very important form of advertising as the ads are huge and are visible to one and all. The important part of the advertising is that the message to be delivered should be crisp and to the point. Though images can be used, but they cannot be used in excess. Everything should be presented to the viewer in such a format so that the viewers make up their mind to buy the product or service.

The message to be delivered can be an ad to buy a product, take a trip, vote for a politician, or give to a charity. According to Outdoor Advertising Association of America (OAAA), millions of dollars are being spent on outdoor advertising each year and the figures are expected to grow. This is due to the fact that outdoor traffic keeps on growing every year and hence the target audience for outdoor advertising is ever increasing.

The print and newspaper advertising takes up a huge part of advertising but outdoor advertising is unique in its own way. It is an extremely cost-effective method of advertising. All you need to do is to design a billboard and get it printed as compared to the television advertising where an entire 30 second commercial has to be designed. If the outdoor ads are strategically placed, it can guarantee substantial exposure for very little cost. That is why outdoor advertising is very cost-effective.

Different industries make use of outdoor advertising in their own different way. For example, eating joints and eateries on the highway make use of highway billboards to draw the customer to have a bite and rest a little at their joint. Mac Donalds and Subway are the excellent examples. The automobile and tourism industries make use of the billboards to advertise their products and tourism plans. These are way too successful because of the fact that people on the highway are on the lookout for such information.

Apart from the billboards, there are several other forms in which outdoor advertising can take place. For example, beverage companies make use of sporting events and arenas to showcase their products. For example, Coca Cola was one of the FIFA World Cup sponsors. Other places where you can see outdoor advertising are:

- taxicabs
- buses
- railways
- subways and walls on which murals are painted

All these forms of outdoor advertising are very popular and extremely cost effective.

The OAAA has divided the Outdoor Advertising into four major categories: Billboards - These usually account for almost half of the revenue of outdoor advertising. Then there is transit system and mobile advertising which also takes up a major pie of outdoor advertising. Advertising on public furniture is also used comprehensively these days globally. Last but not the least is alternative advertising. Such advertising can be in the form of Corporate blogging which is an important form of advertising these days.

To conclude, one can say that outdoor advertising, if used wisely is very powerful and cost-effective way of advertising.

Objectives and Importance of Advertising

Advertising is the best way to communicate to the customers. Advertising helps informs the customers about the brands available in the market and the variety of products useful to them. Advertising is for everybody including kids, young and old. It is done using various media types, with different techniques and methods most suited.

Let us take a look on the main objectives and importance

of advertising.

Objectives of Advertising

Four main Objectives of advertising are:

  i.   Trial

 ii.   Continuity

iii.   Brand switch

iv.   Switching back

Let's take a look on these various types of objectives.

1. **Trial:** the companies which are in their introduction stage generally work for this objective. The trial objective is the one which involves convincing the customers to buy the new product introduced in the market. Here, the advertisers use flashy and attractive ads to make customers take a look on the products and purchase for trials.

2. **Continuity:** this objective is concerned about keeping the existing customers to stick on to the product. The advertisers here generally keep on bringing something new in the product and the advertisement so that the existing customers keep buying their products.

3. **Brand switch:** this objective is basically for those companies who want to attract the customers of the

competitors. Here, the advertisers try to convince the customers to switch from the existing brand they are using to their product.

4. **Switching back:** this objective is for the companies who want their previous customers back, who have switched to their competitors. The advertisers use different ways to attract the customers back like discount sale, new advertise, some reworking done on packaging, etc.

Basically, advertising is a very artistic way of communicating with the customers. The main characteristics one should have to get on their objectives are great communication skills and very good convincing power.

Importance of Advertising

Advertising plays a very important role in today's age of competition. Advertising is one thing which has become a necessity for everybody in today's day to day life, be it the producer, the traders, or the customer. Advertising is an important part. Lets have a look on how and where is advertising important:

1. Advertising is important for the customers

Just imagine television or a newspaper or a radio channel without an advertisement! No, no one can any day imagine this. Advertising plays a very important role in customers life. Customers are the people who buy the product only after they are made aware of the products available in the market. If the product is not advertised, no customer will come to know what products are available and will not buy the product even if the product was for their benefit. One more thing is that advertising helps people find the best products for themselves, their kids, and their family. When they come to know about the range of products, they are able to compare the products and buy so that they get what they desire after spending their valuable money. Thus, advertising is important for the customers.

2. Advertising is important for the seller and companies producing the products

Yes, advertising plays very important role for the producers and the sellers of the products, because

- Advertising helps increasing sales
- Advertising helps producers or the companies to know their competitors and plan accordingly to meet up the level of competition.

- If any company wants to introduce or launch a new product in the market, advertising will make a ground for the product. Advertising helps making people aware of the new product so that the consumers come and try the product.

- Advertising helps creating goodwill for the company and gains customer loyalty after reaching a mature age.

- The demand for the product keeps on coming with the help of advertising and demand and supply become a never ending process.

3. Advertising is important for the society

Advertising helps educating people. There are some social issues also which advertising deals with like child labour, liquor consumption, girl child killing, smoking, family planning education, etc. thus, advertising plays a very important role in society.

Advertising Campaigns - Meaning and its Process

Advertising campaigns are the groups of advertising messages which are similar in nature. They share same messages and themes placed in different types of medias at some fixed times. The time frames of advertising campaigns are fixed and specifically defined.

The very prime thing before making an ad campaign is to know-

Why you are advertising and what are you advertising ?

Why refers to the objective of advertising campaign. The objective of an advertising campaign is to

- Inform people about your product
- Convince them to buy the product
- Make your product available to the customers

The process of making an advertising campaign is as follows:

1. Research: first step is to do a market research for the product to be advertised. One needs to find out the product demand, competitors, etc.

2. Know the target audience: one need to know who are going to buy the product and who should be targeted.

3. Setting the budget: the next step is to set the budget keeping in mind all the factors like media, presentations, paper works, etc which have a role in the process of advertising and the places where there is a need of funds.

4. Deciding a proper theme: the theme for the campaign has to be decided as in the colors to be used, the graphics should be similar or almost similar in all ads, the music and the voices to be used, the designing of the ads, the way the message will be delivered, the language to be used, jingles, etc.

5. Selection of media: the media or number of Medias selected should be the one which will reach the target customers.

6. Media scheduling: the scheduling has to be done accurately so that the ad will be visible or be read or be audible to the targeted customers at the right time.

7. Executing the campaign: finally the campaign has to be executed and then the feedback has to be noted.

Mostly used media tools are print media and electronic media. Print media includes newspaper, magazines, pamphlets, banners, and hoardings. Electronic media includes radio, television, e-mails, sending message on mobiles, and telephonic advertising. The only point to remember is getting a proper frequency for the ad campaign so that the ad is visible and grasping time for customers is good enough.

All campaigns do not have fix duration. Some campaigns are seasonal and some run all year round. All campaigns differ in timings. Some advertising campaigns are media based, some are area based, some are product based, and some are objective based. It is seen that generally advertising campaigns run successfully, but in case if the purpose is not solved in any case, then the theory is redone, required changes are made using the experience, and the remaining campaign is carried forward.

Models of Advertising Scheduling

Scheduling directly refers to the patterns of time in which the advertisement is going to run. It helps fixing up the time slots according to the advertiser so that the message to be delivered will reach target audience in a proper way with proper timings. There are basically three models of advertising scheduling as follows:

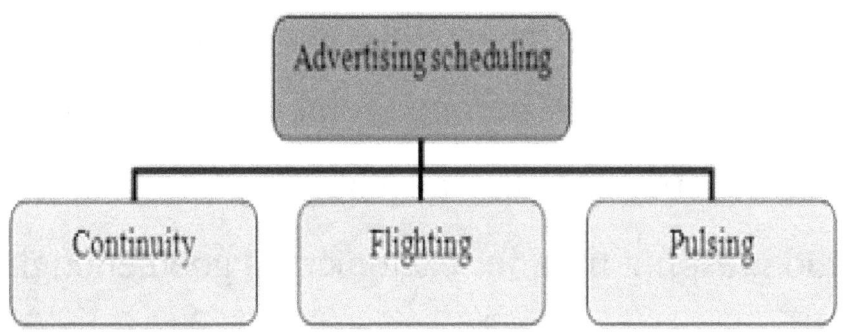

1. **Continuity:** This model is very good option for the products or services which don't depend on season for advertisements. They run ads whole year round. The advertisements under this type run at regular and fixed intervals. The main advantage here is reminding about your products to the customers continuously. This model helps maintain a continuous and complete purchase cycle. This is a best model for the products having continuous demand all the year round. There can be a Rising Continuity in which some specific products are been advertised in the peak seasons for e.g. floaters are advertised more in rainy season while some products fall under a Falling Continuity in which either ads for new products are run or if there is any other change in the existing product. E.g. packaging of Pediasure, a kid's health drink is recently changed.

2. **Flighting:** This model is also called bursting. As the name suggests, this an absolute season based products model. The ads here run at very irregular intervals. Advertisements are for very shorter periods and sometimes no ads at all. The ads are in concentrated forms. So, the biggest advantage here is there is very less

waste of funds as the ads run only at the peak time when the product demand is on high. Television and radio are the most used media types in this method. So the advertisers who cannot afford the year long ads, this is a best option. E.g. ads for warm clothes in Indian Market.

3. **Pulsing:** This model is the combination of both continuity and flighting scheduling. Here, ads run whole year round but at a lower sidxe that means less ads, and heavy advertisements are preferred at the peak time. So this model has advantages of both the other models. Generally scheduling is fixed for a month. There are six types of scheduling method here.

- Steady pulse has fixed schedule for 12 months.
- Seasonal pulse has bunches of ads season wise.
- Period pulse regular basis ads.
- Erratic pulse refers to irregular ads normally used for changing old patterns.
- Start up pulse is used for new product with heavy advertisements.
- Promotional pulse refers to short period single use ads used basically for promoting products or events.

Using this interface, you can set the time periods in which you want to run your campaign. Then click OK button.

Thus, points to remember while scheduling an advertisement are:

- Selecting a proper media type for running ads
- Selecting a correct time for running ads so that the purpose is solved.
- Advertisements should be sufficient enough (in number) to deliver the message to the target.

Industrial Advertising - Business to Business Advertising

The most popular terminology used for industrial advertising is Business to Business advertising. This type of advertising generally includes a company advertising its products or services for the companies which actually uses same or similar products or services or we can say that the advertising company should produce the products which the other company needs for its productions or functions. For e.g. some mineral water companies which work on a smaller scale outsource the packaging bottles, the caps for bottles, the cover with name printed on it, etc. so for this, the advertisements of the manufacturers of bottles, caps and outer packaging paper can work.

A smaller to smaller and largest of all, every company has to do industrial advertising. For e.g. if a company is making coffee powder, it will sell its powder to the distributors who in turn will sale it to the retailers and wholesalers and also to the big companies who has a coffee machine for their employees. Thus companies manufacturing any products can be advertised to the other companies, like raw materials, the machineries used by other companies, spare parts of the machines which makes it work, anything.

Role of Industrial Advertising

- It minimizes the hunt for buyers.
- It helps in increasing sales of the company.
- It helps in making more and more distribution channels.
- It makes company work more efficiently to produce the desired product or service.
- It creates awareness among the customers or other companies about the products and services.

Process of Industrial Advertising

The strategies used in industrial advertising differ from company to company, as different companies have different products to be advertised. So, a single rule cannot work for all the companies' advertisements. But the basic process which can lead to a successful advertisement is: knowing the objective for advertising - identifying the target companies - researching about the market conditions and the competitors - creating the ad to be delivered - selecting media to be used - what should be the budget allotted - execution of the advertisement - getting the feedbacks from the customers.

Media types in Industrial Advertising

The media generally used in the industrial advertising is print media and direct marketing.

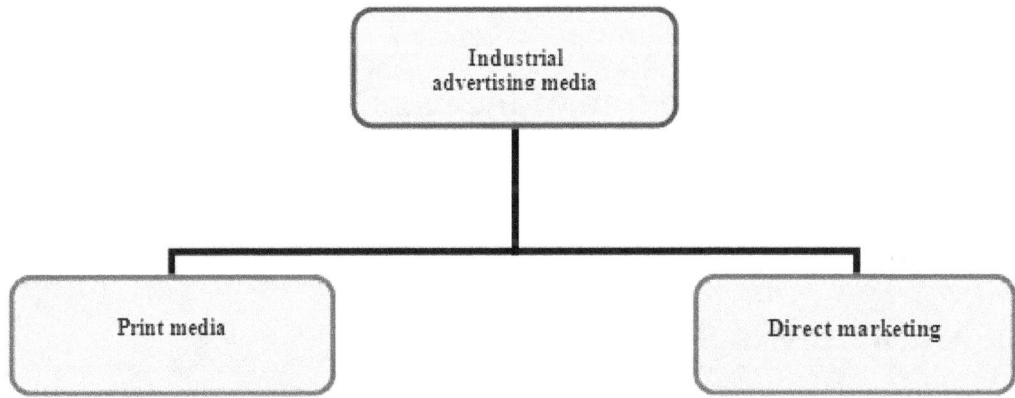

Print Media includes business magazines, trade publications, newspapers, technical journals, etc. To make print media work efficiently, there are some do's and don'ts to be kept in mind:

- Visual image of the ad should be very sharp and prominent

- The ad should be so impressive that readers get attracted towards reading it

- The highlight should be on the service or product offered and not the source by which it is being offered

- Let the ad be simple to be read (with no difficult fonts)

- The picture shown should not be irrelevant with the product.

- The ad should reflect the company's image.

- The ad should to be in logical sequence if it is of two or more pages.

- Headlines should be catchy and suiting the product image.

- And lastly, at the bottom of the page, the company name, address and phone number of the respected office should be mentioned clearly without fail.

Direct Marketing includes:

1. **Direct Mail -** here, the newsletters, data sheets, and the brochures of the company are directly mailed to the customers' postal address.

2. **Telephonic Advertising -** the advertising is done by calling up the customers on there telephones, giving messages on mobile phones, etc.

3. **Online Advertising** - includes companies sending e-mails to the customers or other companies enclosing information about their products ant services, putting online banners, providing e-shopping options, etc.

The advertisers also use other ways for promoting their products like participating in trade shows, trade expos, and fairs.

Thus, the companies can use any or every type of advertising, the important motto being increase in sales, producing best quality products, maintaining good relations with the customers, and achieving the desired goal.

Ethics in Advertising

Ethics means a set of moral principles which govern a person's behavior or how the activity is conducted. And advertising means a mode of communication between a seller and a buyer.

Thus ethics in advertising means a set of well defined principles which govern the ways of communication taking place between the seller and the buyer. Ethics is the most important feature of the advertising industry. Though there are many benefits of advertising but then there are some points which don't match the ethical norms of advertising.

An ethical ad is the one which doesn't lie, doesn't make fake or false claims and is in the limit of decency.

Nowadays, ads are more exaggerated and a lot of puffing is used. It seems like the advertisers lack knowledge of ethical norms and principles. They just don't understand and are unable to decide what is correct and what is wrong.

The main area of interest for advertisers is to increase their sales, gain more and more customers, and increase the demand for the product by presenting a well decorated, puffed and colorful ad. They claim that their product is the best, having unique qualities than the competitors, more cost effective, and more beneficial. But most of these ads are found to be false, misleading customers and unethical. The best example of these types of ads is the one which shows evening snacks for the kids, they use coloring and gluing to make the product look glossy and attractive to the consumers who are watching the ads on television and convince them to buy the product without giving a second thought.

Ethics in Advertising is directly related to the purpose of advertising and the nature of advertising. Sometimes exaggerating the ad becomes necessary to prove the benefit of the product. For e.g. a sanitary napkin ad which shows that when the napkin was dropped in a river by some girls, the napkin soaked whole water of the river. Thus, the purpose of advertising was only to inform women about the product quality. Obviously, every woman knows that this cannot practically happen but the ad was accepted. This doesn't show that the ad was unethical.

Ethics also depends on what we believe. If the advertisers make the ads on the belief that the customers will understand, persuade them to think, and then act on their ads, then this will lead to positive results and the ad may not be called unethical. But at the same time, if advertisers believe that they can fool their customers by showing any impractical things like just clicking fingers will make your home or office fully furnished or just buying a lottery ticket will make you a millionaire, then this is not going to work out for them and will be called as unethical.

Recently, the Vetican issued an article which says ads should follow three moral principles - Truthfulness, Social Responsibility and Upholding Human Dignity.

Generally, big companies never lie as they have to prove their points to various ad regulating bodies. Truth is always said but not completely. Sometimes its better not to reveal the whole truth in the ad but at times truth has to be shown for betterment.

Pharmaceutical Advertising - they help creating awareness, but one catchy point here is that the advertisers show what the medicine can cure but never talk about the side effects of that same thing or the risks involved in intake of it.

Children - children are the major sellers of the ads and the product. They have the power to convince the buyers. But when advertisers are using children in their ad, they should remember not to show them alone doing there work on their own like brushing teeth, playing with toys, or infants holding their own milk bottles as everyone knows that no one will leave their kids unattended while doing all these activities. So showing parents also involved in all activities or things being advertised will be more logical.

Alcohol - till today, there hasn't come any liquor ad which shows anyone drinking the original liquor. They use mineral water and sodas in their advertisements with their brand name. These types of ads are called surrogate ads. These type of ads are totally unethical when liquor ads are totally banned. Even if there are no advertisements for alcohol, people will continue drinking.

Cigarettes and Tobacco - these products should be never advertised as consumption of these things is directly and badly responsible for cancer and other severe health issues. These as are already banned in countries like India, Norway, Thailand, Finland and Singapore.

Ads for social causes - these types of ads are ethical and are accepted by the people. But ads like condoms and contraceptive pills should be limited, as these are sometimes unethical, and are more likely to loose morality and decency at places where there is no educational knowledge about all these products.

Looking at all these above mentioned points, advertisers should start taking responsibility of self regulating their ads by:

- design self regulatory codes in their companies including ethical norms, truth, decency, and legal points
- keep tracking the activities and remove ads which don't fulfill the codes.
- Inform the consumers about the self regulatory codes of the company

- Pay attention on the complaints coming from consumers about the product ads.

- Maintain transparency throughout the company and system.

When all the above points are implemented, they will result in:

- making the company answerable for all its activities

- will reduce the chances of getting pointed out by the critics or any regulatory body.

- will help gain confidence of the customers, make them trust the company and their products.

Measuring Advertising Effectiveness

"When a child writes the examination papers, he has to see the result come what it may be, so that he comes to know where he is wrong and where he should pay more attendance. This will help him work better in future."

This is exactly the case of the advertisement. The work is not complete if the effectiveness of advertise is not measured. This is the only way to know how the advertisement is performing, is it reaching the targets and is the goal achieved. It is not at all possible to measure advertisement effectiveness accurately as there are many factors like making a brand image, increasing the sales, keeping people informed about the product, introducing new product, etc, which affect the effectiveness of an advertisement.

We all know that there are some companies who advertise at very low level but still their products are a hit and some companies indulge in very heavy advertisements but they don't get desirable results. But then, there are some traditional and modern tools to measure most of the effectiveness of an advertisement through which the advertiser can or may get more and more information about how their ads and product are performing in the market. According to Philip Kotler and Armstrong, the Gurus Of Marketing, there are two most popular areas which need to be measured for knowing the effectiveness of advertisement and they are:

- Communication Effect
- Sales Effect

Communication Effect Research consists of three types of researches:

1. **Direct Rating Method -** here, customers are directly asked to rate the advertisement and then these rating are calculated.

2. **Portfolio Tests -** here, the customers see the ads and listen carefully to the ads and all the contents of the ads and then they are asked to recall the ad and the contents. Then the calculations are done with help of this data.

3. **Laboratory tests -** here, the apparatus to measure the heart rates, blood pressure, perspiration, etc are used on the customer after he watches the ad, to know the physiological reactions of the body.

Sales Effect Research totally depends on the sales of the company. The sales keep varying from time to time. There are some factors affecting sales like product availability, the price of the product, contents of the product, and sometimes the competitors. So this method is a little difficult than the communication one. The company doing sales effect research generally bothers about the sales of the product, they try to know whether or not the money they are spending on the ads is enough or excess.

As earlier said, it is not possible to measure each and everything and the chances are at the lower end if the company has many ads running through various mediums at the same time. So suggestion is that the advertiser or the company should use appropriate and different methods which are most suitable for the media under use.

- The company can hold surveys and product recognition tests

- Questionnaire or feedback flyers can be distributed and customers could be asked to fill it up.

- Toll free number can be highlighted on the ads so that customers can call up.

- The response rates can be increased by telling customers what to do. For e.g. some ads have lines in flashy color like "Hurry Up" or "No one can eat just one" or "be the first" etc.

These are the traditional ways. Now days, internet is the modern tool for measuring the effectiveness of an advertisement. There are some types such as:

Integrated direct marketing - This is an internet based tool where they have a response corner designed on the websites. Whenever the customers visit the sites, they fill up their contact details and give feedbacks. Thus the company supplies more information and sends newsletters and also gets the idea for further action. But then its not that only online advertiser have this facility but then advertisers who don't work online can use coupons, discount vouchers, etc. to do this.

Analysis tool - there is an analysis tool available on internet by using which the advertiser will know how many customers are visiting the site, who are shopping online, how many pages are viewed, etc. which in turn will help advertiser to measure the effectiveness.

Internet is the most easy, cheaper and cost effective way to measure the effectiveness because here no money is wasted as the ad is only viewed when the customer want to view it where as in normal print method or using TV, the ad sometimes goes unwatched or unattended and viewed for the sake of viewing.

Advertising Myths - Ifs and Buts of the Advertising Industry

Advertising is considered as the best tool to make people aware of the product a company wants to sell. This is the best way to communicate with the audience and to inform them about the product but with a proper media selection and of course timing. But there are some myths which have been creating problems in the path of successful advertising. We have tried to clarify some misinterpretations about the ifs and buts of the advertising industry.

Advertising Myths

1. **Advertising works only for some business Wrong.** Advertising works for each and every company or business it only it is executed properly. But due to bad advertising, many ad campaigns fail to work in desired way and the people think that advertisements are not their cup of tea. They must understand one simple rule of advertising - it should be for right people at right time through right medium on right place.

2. **Advertising is only needed when business is slow** Wrong. Who said that the big and successful brands don't advertise their products? Advertising is a continuous process with some renovations whenever needed. But, yes, when the business really is going slow or at its low, the advertising will have to be heavy and more in number. This will help the product to improve its market value and make people aware of the product.

3. If the product is not selling, advertise it

This is just not true. Just think about it. If you are selling a product which is not at all in vogue, and no one is using it, how will it get clear from the shelf. You need to understand the need of customers and then sell the product. Advertise doesn't mean selling anything you want but it means selling what customers wants.

4. Advertise creates needs

No. The people already had cassettes to play and listen to music they liked when they didn't have the option of CDs. It is technology which came in, and it was only then CDs were advertised and sold. Advertise only replaces the old things with new, it doesn't creates needs.

5. Advertise effects persist for decades

It's the quality of the product which persists. Advertise no doubt helps increasing sales of the product and stays in memory of the people, but minds are captured by the product itself.

6. Humuor in ads

Sometimes humour gets in the way of delivering message properly to the consumers but not every time it creates problems. Many of the times it helps people to remember the ad and the product and helps creating a positive attitude towards the advertise.

7. Sex sells

Not always. Some advertisers use sex for just increasing the sales and forget that the product doesn't need this type of ad at all. Remember once models Milind Soman and Madhu Sapre posed naked for a shoe brand. It was really irrelevant.

8. Creativity is the most important factor

The ad should be no doubt creative enough to attract consumers but it not the only selling factor. There has to be good message to deliver, best media selection, and best quality of the product to make the product and ad both successful.

9. Advertising costs so much

Advertise needs money but one has to also consider the results in forms of increased sales, increased reputation in industry, recognition for product and also increased market value of product which advertisements brings along. Lets consider advertising as investment and not expense.

Thus these are the most common myths of the ad industry which are working as hurdles in the way of bright future of advertisers and advertising and we need to overcome these hurdles and rise.

Future of Advertising

Advertising is still all about the 'ifs and buts of a product', presented in a glowing rainbow like picture trying to attract consumers….but what is the future of advertising in coming years ?

Lets go way back when the idea of advertising a product was regarded as some kind of a big deal. Then the advertisements were very limited, and it took lots and lots of efforts to make a single advertisement. And the customers then, had no option other than watching those advertisements. Now, time has changed. Since last 20 years or lets just consider last 10 years, there has been a dramatic change in the world of advertisement. And this will not have a stopage in coming years. The change doesn't mean that the advertising agencies will all be shut down and firms will take over. It just means that the existing advertising agencies will have to experience a change in the industry and within. They will be redefined and reinvented so that they can survive in the years ahead. The agencies which gave their number of years to this industry will also change for good, be capable to cope up with new challenges, new competition and new attitudes of the consumers. Once a article was written on change in advertising in 1992 and the title then also suits now, it said - Advertising Age : Change or Die and very well said. To understand what is going to change and what will remain the same should be on the top of the list of the advertisers.

Now is the beginning of the digital era. The agencies had a system of having some few creative people who used to come with ideas for ads. That was the time when giving an ad in radio and television was very expensive. But now no one minds actually about the cost for such ads because consumers are responding well. But now and onwards, internet and technology has taken a front seat. Lets talk about the mass media. Today every tv serial, all movies running in theatres and all breaks in the radio channels have fillers called ads. But in the coming years, the ads can be shown to the consumers only if they want to see and not because the advertiser want them to see it. The cost of using internet and digital gadgets is everyday dropping down so the customers don't mind spending on these things other that fooling themselves with the colorful advertisements. The future will be in favour of the advertisers and advertisements but only at the cost of proper management and proper use of digital technologies and internet.

The Bond

Nowdays, no one trusts the ad industry because there is no transparency. The ethics are not being the part of ads anymore. In coming years, the bond of trust has to be again rebuilt between the consumers and the advertisers. The advertisers will have to work hard to gain the confidence of the customers.

More Creativity

The creative people of the agencies should not limit their creativity by only working with the old style menu. This is the time to explore with help of internet and digital tools.

Differentiated Products

The advertisers should launch a product which will be completely different but excellent to use. Then only the voice will be heard.

Attract Talent

More and more quality people should be hired today who will

be leaders for tomorrow. They will be the people who will lead the industry in the future with the best quality being coping up will everything. Better HR practices should also be appointed.

These are some points which may help advertisers to survive and survive in a better way in the future. The people who will not change can just not stay in this new industry.

www.ingramcontent.com/pod-product-compliance
Lightning Source LLC
Chambersburg PA
CBHW080820180526
45168CB00006B/2516